T0219612

Introducing
Jakarta EE CDI

Contexts and Dependency Injection for Enterprise Java Development

Luqman Saeed

Apress®

Introducing Jakarta EE CDI: Contexts and Dependency Injection for Enterprise Java Development

Luqman Saeed
Accra, Ghana

ISBN-13 (pbk): 978-1-4842-5641-1   ISBN-13 (electronic): 978-1-4842-5642-8
https://doi.org/10.1007/978-1-4842-5642-8

Managing Director, Apress Media LLC: Welmoed Spahr
Acquisitions Editor: Steve Anglin
Development Editor: Matthew Moodie
Coordinating Editor: Mark Powers

Cover designed by eStudioCalamar

Cover image designed by Freepik (www.freepik.com)

Distributed to the book trade worldwide by Apress Media, LLC, 1 New York Plaza, New York, NY 10004, U.S.A. Phone 1-800-SPRINGER, fax (201) 348-4505, e-mail orders-ny@springer-sbm.com, or visit www.springeronline.com. Apress Media, LLC is a California LLC and the sole member (owner) is Springer Science + Business Media Finance Inc (SSBM Finance Inc). SSBM Finance Inc is a **Delaware** corporation.

For information on translations, please e-mail editorial@apress.com; for reprint, paperback, or audio rights, please email bookpermissions@springernature.com.

Apress titles may be purchased in bulk for academic, corporate, or promotional use. eBook versions and licenses are also available for most titles. For more information, reference our Print and eBook Bulk Sales web page at http://www.apress.com/bulk-sales.

Any source code or other supplementary material referenced by the author in this book is available to readers on GitHub via the book's product page, located at www.apress.com/9781484256411. For more detailed information, please visit http://www.apress.com/source-code.

Printed on acid-free paper

Table of Contents

About the Author

Luqman Saeed is a Java EE developer with Pedantic Devs. He has been in software development for close to a decade. He started with PHP and now does Java EE full time. His goal on Udemy is to help you get productive with powerful, modern, intuitive, and easy-to-use Java EE APIs. He will provide you with the best of vanilla, pure, and awesome Java EE courses to help you master the skills needed to solve whatever development challenge you have at hand.

About the Technical Reviewer

Chád ("Shod") Darby is an author, instructor, and speaker in the Java development world. As a recognized authority on Java applications and architectures, he has presented technical sessions at software development conferences worldwide (in the United States, UK, India, Russia, and Australia). In his 15 years as a professional software architect, he's had the opportunity to work for Blue Cross/Blue Shield, Merck, Boeing, Red Hat, and a handful of start-up companies.

Chád is a contributing author to several Java books, including *Professional Java E-Commerce* (Wrox Press), *Beginning Java Networking* (Wrox Press), and *XML and Web Services Unleashed* (Sams Publishing). Chád has Java certifications from Sun Microsystems and IBM. He holds a BS in computer science from Carnegie Mellon University. You can visit Chád's blog at `www.luv2code.com` to view his free video tutorials on Java. You can also follow him on Twitter at `@darbyluvs2code`.

Preface

Thank you for picking up *Introducing Jakarta EE CDI: Contexts and Dependency Injection for Enterprise Java Development.* I wrote this book as a response to the lack of easy-to-understand books on using the compelling and intuitive Contexts and Dependency Injection API on the Jakarta EE (formerly Java EE) platform.

This book covers the very essentials of the CDI API and aims at explaining the various constructs in a way that is easy to understand and relate to. The ultimate goal is to help you, the everyday Java developer, write better code. Throughout the book, you will be working on a simple restaurant application, seeing when and how the various CDI API constructs can be used.

What Do You Need to Know to Use This Book?

Ideally, you should be a Java developer who is comfortable with Java SE before starting with this book. Knowing a bit of Java EE or Spring should help you pick up the concepts faster, but isn't required. You should also have at least Java 8 installed on your machine.

What Does the Book Cover?

The book starts with the theory of Java EE, including its evolution to present-day Jakarta EE, and proceeds to cover CDI, starting with how to activate it explicitly. The discussion then builds on the concept of CDI beans and discusses the various types. You then learn about CDI contexts and injection points. The book then introduces CDI qualifiers, producers, interceptors, and finally CDI events.

What Will You Learn in the End?

This is a very concise book that covers only what matters. Your time is important, so I selected topics that I use personally in my day-to-day coding. There is no point in loading the book with topics you will only use sparingly. So this book should be straightforward to consume over a weekend.

At the end of this book, you will have a firm grasp of the Contexts and Dependency Injection API. You'll know what it is, when to use it, and how to write better, more readable and maintainable code with it.

Where Is the Source Code?

The entire code for the book is available on GitHub, both in an Apress branded repo located at www.github.com/apress/introducing-jakarta-ee-cdi and on my own repo, located at https://github.com/pedanticdev/jee-book. The project is built with the Maven dependency management tool and should work in any IDE that supports Maven. If you do not have Maven installed, you can follow the guide found at https://www.baeldung.com/install-maven-on-windows-linux-mac to install it on your machine. It is available for all OSes out there. I highly encourage you to clone the code to your local machine to follow along with the book.

The project object model (pom.xml) file contains the Payara Micro Maven plugin that you can use to run the code sample. Change to the project directory and issue the following command:

```
mvn package payara-micro:start
```

To get the Async CDI events running, you will need to download the Payara Server Full Stream from `www.payara.fish/software/downloads/` and follow the video found at `www.youtube.com/watch?v=aw-cNxKJU_Y` to run the cloned code.

How Do You Reach Me?

Writing a book is a tedious task, and as such, despite best efforts, there may be errors that escape through quality checks. I take full responsibility for all of them.

Should you encounter any such errors, need help with anything in this book, or just want to hang out for coffee, please do not hesitate to reach out to me personally via `hello@pedanticacademy.com`.

Once again, thank you for picking up this book. I hope you write better code after reading it. Let's get started.

—Luqman Saeed

CHAPTER 1

What Is Java EE?

At its core, the Java Enterprise Edition (Java EE), formerly known as J2EE, is a collection of *abstract, standardized specifications* that prescribe solutions to commonly faced challenges in software development.

It is important to note the word *abstract* in this definition. This means that Java EE is simply a set of interfaces and contracts that provide a public-facing API for developers.

These abstract specs are also said to be *standardized*. What does that mean? It means that the entire collection of Java EE APIs are published according to well-defined criteria set by experts in the subject field of the API[1].

By standardized, it also means that every Java EE API has gone through the rigorous process of the Java Community Process's Java Spec Request program. The result of this process is a set of APIs that are industry-tried and -tested and are deemed to be here to stay.

However, remember that I said Java EE is abstract, right? Well, even though you will generally code against the Java EE APIs in the `javax.*` packages, you can't run your application on Java EE per se.

---

[1]https://jcp.org/en/eg/eghome

L. Saeed, *Introducing Jakarta EE CDI*, https://doi.org/10.1007/978-1-4842-5642-8_1

How Do You Run a Java EE App?

To run a Java EE application, you need a concrete implementation of the Java EE spec. Remember that they are abstract. The official name given to the concrete implementation of Java EE is an *application server*. I bet you have heard that phrase before, right?

An application server is basically a concrete implementation of the Java EE abstract specs. This means that you run your application code using Java EE API implementations on an application server.

There are many application servers out there, including Payara Server, Apache TomEE, JBoss Wildfly, and IBM OpenLiberty, among others.

CHAPTER 2

What Is a Java Specification Request (JSR)?

At its core, a Java Specification Request is a formal, open standard document proposal that is made by an individual or organization to the Java Community Process (JCP)[1]. It contains proposed changes, additions, or improvements to the Java technology platform.

Many essential points can be gleaned from this definition. First is that a JSR is a formal document. What this means is that a JSR or a request for adding to the Java technology group must take a certain predefined format. This format is defined by the JCP.

Also, a JSR is an open standard document. What this means, again, is that a JSR is a document that conforms to certain established rules and regulations regarding its distribution and contributions to it. It also means that whatever is contained in the JSR is easily accessible to anyone interested in assessing it.

Flowing from the definition of a Java Specification Request is that a JSR can be made by either an individual or organization. Any member of the JCP can make a JSR. JCP membership is opened to the public; it's free for

---

[1]https://jcp.org/en/home/index

© Luqman Saeed 2020
L. Saeed, *Introducing Jakarta EE CDI*, https://doi.org/10.1007/978-1-4842-5642-8_2

individuals as well. So what this means is that you cannot make a request to the JCP without being a member of the organization.

Finally, a JSR is a document that proposes changes, additions, or improvements to the Java technology platform. Every JSR contains new features, bug fixes, or general improvements, in one way or the other, to the Java technology stack.

Every major API available on Java EE is actually a JSR specification that has gone through the process of being approved by the JCP. All JSRs have a process they have to go through to be approved by the JCP.

Once a JSR is approved by the JCP, it becomes part of the Java stack and can be safely used in production. The JSR process ensures that only well tested technologies become part of the Java stack, preventing unnecessary bloat in the form of fad technologies.

The JSR process also ensures that APIs are carefully crafted in such a way as to preserve backward compatibility. If there is one thing Java is known for, it's backward compatibility, and the JSR process ensures that this crucial Java feature is maintained.

As a JSR is just an abstract specification, it needs some form of implementation to be useful. That is where the concept of reference implementation (covered in Chapter 3) comes in.

CHAPTER 3

What Is a Reference Implementation?

In the previous chapter, you learned what a JSR is. Recall that a JSR is an abstract request to the JCP that contains proposed additions to the Java technology platform.

Because it is abstract, you cannot run it. A JSR needs to have some form of implementation, or concrete realization, to be useful to end developers. That is where the concept of *reference implementation* comes in.

Every JSR must have a reference implementation, which is a concrete implementation of the specification contained in the JSR document. This is a requirement of the JCP. Every single JSR has a reference implementation that is freely available and bundled with the application servers.

A JSR also has a Technology Compatibility Kit (TCK), which is "a suite of tests that at least nominally checks a particular alleged implementation of a Java Specification Request (JSR) for compliance."[1]

A TCK is used to test a JSR implementation for compliance with the spec. That is part of why Java EE is said to be a *standardized* set of specifications.

---

[1]https://en.wikipedia.org/wiki/Technology_Compatibility_Kit

© Luqman Saeed 2020
L. Saeed, *Introducing Jakarta EE CDI*, https://doi.org/10.1007/978-1-4842-5642-8_3

This rigorous process also ensures the quality of the APIs that are derived from the JSR document. Some popular reference implementations (RIs) of JSRs include the following:

- JSR 380 (Bean Validation 2.0) – Hibernate Validator 6

- JSR 367 (JSON-B Binding) – Eclipse Yasson 1.0

- JSR 370 (JAX-RS 2.1) – Jersey

- JSR 365 (CDI 2.0) – WELD 3.0

These are some of the new and more popular JSRs and their respective reference implementations. Most of these reference implementations are bundled with application servers, which is the subject of the next chapter.

CHAPTER 4

What Is an Application Server?

The previous chapter talked about what a JSR reference implementation is. The definition of Java EE also mentioned that it is a collection of abstract specifications. Java EE itself is a Java Specification Request.

Better still, Java EE is what is termed an *umbrella JSR* in that it encapsulates some JSRs. So Java EE 7, for instance, is JSR 342. Java EE 8 is JSR 366. So Java EE itself is a JSR that goes through the JCP JSR process and is subject to the requirements of every JSR.

Flowing from this idea and remembering that the JSR process requires every JSR to have a reference implementation, this means Java EE as an umbrella JSR must also have a reference implementation.

The implementation of the umbrella JSR or Java EE is commonly referred to as an *application server*. An app server is a concrete implementation of the Java EE spec that you can actually run your code on. The reference implementation of Java EE is the Glassfish Application Server.

An application server generally abstracts the developer away from a lot of mundane stuff that you would have had to manage on your own, like data-source pooling, caching, clustering, and other overheads.

© Luqman Saeed 2020
L. Saeed, *Introducing Jakarta EE CDI*, https://doi.org/10.1007/978-1-4842-5642-8_4

The application server must also pass the TCK to be fully certified as being compliant with the given umbrella JSR. An app server is also the basis for the portability of Java EE. As a developer, you generally are encouraged to code against the `javax.*` packages, which are the standard Java EE packages.

Because an app server is subject to a standard, using the Java EE package means you can swap out application servers and your code will generally run with little to no modifications. This is compelling if you think about it.

For starters, no single application vendor can lock you in. Because you can swap out application servers, you can theoretically change vendors at any time should you be dissatisfied with your current vendor.

There are many application vendors out there, some free, some costly. Popular among the open source ones is Payara Server (see `http://payara.fish`), a Glassfish-derived, fully patched application server that is freely available for download.

Java EE is an abstract spec and its concrete realization or implementation is called an *application server*. As a JSR, the required reference implementation of Java EE is the Glassfish Application Server.

CHAPTER 5

What Is Jakarta EE?

You have learned what Java EE is. You've seen what an application server is and how it relates to the term Java EE. Now it's time to consider what Jakarta EE is.

Jakarta EE is the new Java EE. Back in 2017, Oracle, which was the owner of the Java EE technology stack, decided to open the platform to the wider community. In the process, the entire Java EE platform had to be moved to a non-profit, community-oriented foundation.

The Java EE community voted and chose the Eclipse Foundation. So Java EE was moved to the Eclipse Foundation. Due to legal issues, the name of the platform had to be changed to something other than its original Java EE. Again, the community made suggestions and eventually the name *Jakarta EE* won[1].

With a renewed goal of aligning the former Java EE platform to more modern software development paradigms, the Eclipse Foundation is seeking to position Jakarta EE as a modern, cloud-native, agile software development platform.

One of the criticisms leveled against Java EE was that it was too slow to evolve. The software development landscape moved faster than the platform could keep up. In light of such valid concerns, the Eclipse Foundation, through the Jakarta EE working group, developed the following guiding principles for Jakarta EE:

---

[1]https://eclipse-foundation.blog/2018/02/26/and-the-name-is/

© Luqman Saeed 2020
L. Saeed, *Introducing Jakarta EE CDI*, https://doi.org/10.1007/978-1-4842-5642-8_5

- Deliver more frequent releases

- Provide lower barriers to participation

- Develop the community

- Manage the Jakarta EE brand on behalf of the community

Initially, Jakarta EE is the exact equivalent to the Java EE 8 platform. All of the specifications, reference implementations (RIs), and technology compatibility kits (TCKs) that comprised Java EE 8 have been transferred to the Eclipse Foundation[2]. This means that the former Java EE 8 release is the foundation of the new cloud-native Jakarta EE.

Previous chapters discussed how Java EE evolved through the concept of Java Specification Requests (JSRs) through the Java Community Process (JCP). However, how will Jakarta EE evolve at the Eclipse Foundation? Alternatively, how is the Jakarta EE governance model different from that of Java EE?

The main difference is that the Jakarta EE governance model is now community-based, multi-vendor, and open to participation and contribution by the enterprise consumers of these technologies. The Eclipse Foundation will ensure that the new specifications and development processes for Jakarta EE will remain open, vendor-neutral, and provide a level playing field for all participants.

The Java Community Process (JCP) will be replaced by the Eclipse Foundation Specification Process (EFSP) (see `https://www.eclipse.org/projects/efsp/`). How is it different from the JCP?

---

[2]`https://jakarta.ee/about/faq/`

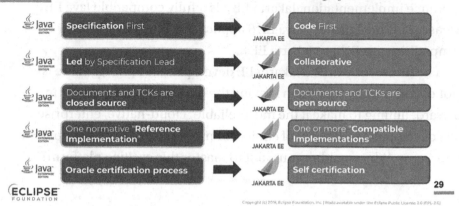

Image Credit

It uses a code-first approach. The most vital difference between the JCP and EFSP is that specifications are going to be developed through this code-first approach. In the JCP, the specification is developed, followed by the reference implementation. In the EFSP, however, there will be hands-on coding and experimenting first to ensure that something is worthy of being included in a specification document.

The other differences all bring more openness on the side of the EFSP than on the erstwhile JCP process. This is a good thing. It means you as a developer can feel safe in using the Jakarta EE platform for your applications, knowing that it is a fully open platform run by a non-profit organization, with broader participation by the entire Java community. Microsoft and Pivotal (the company behind the Spring Framework) are members of the Jakarta EE community.

With regards to releases, the first release of the umbrella specification under Eclipse Foundation is Glassfish 5.1, which is a Java EE 8 compatible release. Recall that Chapter 3 stated that the Glassfish Application Server is the reference implementation of the Java EE umbrella JSR.

The Foundation has released Jakarta EE 8 with Glassfish 5.2 as the reference implementation. Jakarta EE 8 is a fully compatible Java EE 8 release. This means every Java EE 8 application is automatically compatible with Eclipse Jakarta EE 8.

The future for you as a Jakarta EE developer is inspiring. There is a lot of community interest in moving the entire Jakarta EE platform forward, aiming to make it the most reliable, cloud-native, enterprise Java development platform of choice for modern software development paradigms. Why wouldn't you want to master this exciting platform?

CHAPTER 6

Why Jakarta EE?

As a Java developer, you have many choices when it comes to frameworks and platforms for software development. A question you might be asking yourself is why you should choose Jakarta EE as your primary software development platform. What makes it a better choice?

There are number of reasons to at least give Jakarta EE a try, key among them being these:

- Standardization
- Openness
- Stability
- Ease of development
- Portability
- Pick and choose: tank or pistol
- Amazing documentation

Standardization

Every single JSR has gone through a rigorous process of both public and JSR Expert Group scrutiny before being voted on by the JCP EC, for all Java EE APIs. Every JSR is weighed in terms of backward compatibility, benefit to the Java platform as a whole, etc. This painstaking JSR approval process ensures that every feature is accepted based on certain well-defined

© Luqman Saeed 2020
L. Saeed, *Introducing Jakarta EE CDI*, https://doi.org/10.1007/978-1-4842-5642-8_6

technical criteria. Similarly, every API of the new Jakarta EE platform will go through a well-defined specification process to ensure whatever API is included in the platform is going to be there for the long haul.

Openness

As discussed earlier, the new Jakarta EE specifications are going to be developed using a code-first approach through the Eclipse Foundation Specification Process. The EFSP is an open process that anyone can be part of. The entire specification process is developed in the open.

Ease of Development

Jakarta EE development is effortless. All that's needed is an application server or a Jakarta EE compliant runtime and one Maven dependency. It requires minimal configuration, follows convention over configuration, and leads to no XML hell. It also has sensible defaults. For example, EJBs are transactional by default, use default data-source, and are CDI-enabled by default.

```
1 <dependency>
2    <groupId>javax</groupId>
3    <artifactId>javaee-api</artifactId>
4    <version>8.0</version>
5    <scope>provided</scope>
6 </dependency>
7
```

This code snippet is the only dependency you need to have the entire Jakarta EE platform available at your fingertips. Moreover, because you are abstracted from the implementation of the standard, you only package your application with your code and any other third-party libraries used. Your chosen application server will provide the implementation and all the other heavy lifting required to run an application.

Portability

Jakarta EE as a standard means that your application should work with minimal to no configuration across various implementations of the standard, as long as you code against the standard. This is compelling because you don't get locked into one Jakarta EE application runtime vendor. Your code is portable across various application servers as long as you use the standard Jakarta EE APIs.

Pick and Choose: Tank or Pistol

Jakarta EE is a huge platform that may appear intimidating at first. However, you can pick and choose whatever API your application requires. You can use the platform as a tank or as a pistol—you decide. All the various APIs are integrated as a whole if you choose to use Jakarta EE as a tank, or they can stand alone individually if you choose to nitpick. Also, as the application server provides the runtime implementation, whether you choose to use the entire platform or just select APIs, you still ship your application with just your code. Either way, your application is always shipped as a lightweight bundle.

Java EE 8

Batch	Dependency Injection	JACC	JAXR	JSTL	Management
Bean Validation	Deployment	JASPIC	JMS	JTA	Servlet
CDI	EJB	JAX-RPC	JSF	JPA	Web Services
Common Annotations	EL	JAX-RS	JSON-P	JavaMail	Web Services Metadata
Concurrency EE	Interceptors	JAX-WS	JSP	Managed Beans	WebSocket
Connector	JSP Debugging	JAXB			
JSON-B	Security				

Image Credit

Amazing Documentation

Jakarta EE is a well organized community project that has an amazing amount of documentation. Chief among this is the *Java EE Tutorials*[1], the official Java EE handbook. There are also lots of community and corporate organized conferences—like Devoxx and Oracle CodeOne—that place a lot of emphasis on server-side Java development. There are also books written by individual developers like this one you are reading, all focused on helping you become a well-grounded enterprise Java software developer.

These points are just a few of the reasons why you should give Jakarta EE a try. I know in the J2EE days, the platform was a unwieldy thing for a lot of people. However, today, Jakarta EE is a nimble, elegant, deceptively simple but compelling software development platform, as you will see in the second part of this book.

---

[1]https://javaee.github.io/tutorial/

CHAPTER 7

Jakarta EE and the Spring Framework

A book on Jakarta EE would not be complete without a discussion of the Spring Framework. So what is the Spring Framework?

The Spring Framework is an alternative server-side software development platform for the JVM that runs on a servlet container. It used to be Java-based but you can now develop Spring apps with other JVM-based languages like Kotlin. The Spring Framework came about because of the frustrations developers faced using the earlier versions of Java EE, then called J2EE.

Rod Johnson[1] started the project as an alternative platform that was more developer friendly and less arcane than J2EE. In the beginning, the Spring Framework was just an inversion of control (dependency injection) framework. It soon became very popular and has since grown to become a full-stack alternative to Jakarta EE. The Spring Framework intellectual property is owned by Pivotal Inc.

---

[1]https://en.wikipedia.org/wiki/Rod_Johnson_(programmer)

© Luqman Saeed 2020
L. Saeed, *Introducing Jakarta EE CDI*, https://doi.org/10.1007/978-1-4842-5642-8_7

However, as Spring was growing, developers started experiencing pain points that caused them lots of frustrations with the platform[2]. At the same time that Spring was enjoying all the popularity, Java EE was also evolving with all the feedback it was getting.

The release of Java EE 7 marked a milestone in the history of the platform, because it had almost caught up with the Spring Framework in terms of developer productivity, but had managed to avoid Spring's pitfalls. Java EE releases have been heavily influenced by the Spring Framework.

Today, Spring as a platform has the Spring Boot framework, a framework I like to call "Little Java EE for Spring". Spring Boot has been influenced by Java EE's convention over configuration and sensible default philosophies. Both platforms have been very influential of the other.

As a Java developer, you have the choice of using Jakarta EE or the Spring Framework. Neither, for me, is superior to the other. Both platforms have their strengths and weaknesses. Naturally, as the author of a Jakarta EE book, I choose Jakarta EE, but that is because I am excited about its future as an Eclipse Foundation community project, I feel effective using it, and I find it easy to learn and to teach.

You should choose a platform based on its technical merits to you, how easily you can maintain your apps, how much you value backward compatibility, the existing skillset of your development team, and other such metrics. My opinion about the whole Spring vs. Java EE flame wars is that it's just not worth it. They are both excellent platforms that cater to different kinds of developers. Pivotal, the company behind the Spring Framework, is now a member of the Jakarta EE community.

Spring Framework vs. Java EE can be rephrased as Spring Framework *and* Jakarta EE. You as a developer should pick what is right in your context. As you are reading this book, I am certain you have already decided which you want to go with.

---

[2]Why I Hate Spring: http://samatkinson.com/why-i-hate-spring/

CHAPTER 8

The Contexts and Dependency Injection (CDI) API

Dependency injection (DI) is a way of developing software such that various components are related in a very loosely coupled way. In most software applications, there is always some form of dependency between the various bits and pieces.

Take a restaurant application for instance. You might have a component that handles taking orders, another for sending a message to the kitchen, yet another for checking available ingredients for a given meal, and one or two for calculating the total bill.

These are all various components that need to depend on each other to fulfill the duty of running a restaurant. However, creating and managing this inter-dependency can be a difficult task. You need to create individual dependencies for each component, and at times, think of the contexts within which you want a specific dependency to exist.

This is where the concept of dependency injection comes in. With DI, your various components simply declare a dependency on other components and leave the creation, management, and destruction of these dependencies to an external mechanism. In short, you invert control in your application. Components simply request a dependency and some

© Luqman Saeed 2020
L. Saeed, *Introducing Jakarta EE CDI*, https://doi.org/10.1007/978-1-4842-5642-8_8

black box makes that dependency available. That black box is generally referred to as an inversion of control (IoC) container.

Dependency injection is a specific type of IoC "which concerns itself with decoupling dependencies between high-level and low-level layers through shared abstractions."[1] Contexts and Dependency Injection (CDI) is an implementation of the DI principle.

CDI Activation

On the Jakarta EE platform, the API that helps you glue together the disparate components of your application code is the Contexts and Dependency Injection (CDI) API. In its version 2.0, CDI is activated by default in Jakarta EE with the discovery mode set to annotated.

What the default activation scope means is that only beans (or Java classes) annotated with CDI annotations or CDI recognized annotations are eligible for injection. The default CDI config file, a small XML file called beans.xml in the /webapp/WEB-INF folder, looks as shown here:

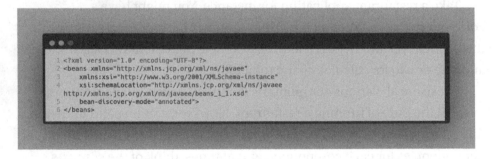

```
1 <?xml version="1.0" encoding="UTF-8"?>
2 <beans xmlns="http://xmlns.jcp.org/xml/ns/javaee"
3     xmlns:xsi="http://www.w3.org/2001/XMLSchema-instance"
4     xsi:schemaLocation="http://xmlns.jcp.org/xml/ns/javaee
http://xmlns.jcp.org/xml/ns/javaee/beans_1_1.xsd"
5     bean-discovery-mode="annotated">
6 </beans>
```

Line 5 is the default bean discovery mode, where bean discovery mode is simply the scanning mechanism for identifying beans that are eligible to be managed by the CDI container. Annotated means only classes with bean defining annotations will be discovered during scanning.

---

[1]https://en.wikipedia.org/wiki/Inversion_of_control

This implies that the following bean will be scanned at application boot time.

```java
 1  @ApplicationScoped
 2  public class TableService {
 3
 4      private final Collection<TableNum> assignedTables = new HashSet<>
 5  ();
 6
 7      public boolean assignTable(TableNum tableNum) {
 8          return assignedTables.add(tableNum);
 9      }
10
11      public boolean checkTableAvailability(TableNum tableNum) {
12          return assignedTables.contains(tableNum);
13      }
14  }
```

However, this class will not be scanned for lack of a bean defining annotation.

```java
 1
 2  public class TableService {
 3
 4      private final Collection<TableNum> assignedTables = new HashSet<>
 5  ();
 6
 7      public boolean assignTable(TableNum tableNum) {
 8          return assignedTables.add(tableNum);
 9      }
10
11      public boolean checkTableAvailability(TableNum tableNum) {
12          return assignedTables.contains(tableNum);
13      }
14  }
```

Note that this is the kind of beans.xml file that kicks in when there isn't an explicitly created file.

Using the CDI API with the default bean discovery mode set to annotated isn't quite fun, however. To utilize the power of Jakarta EE dependency injection fully, you want to set the bean discovery mode to All.

```
1 <?xml version="1.0" encoding="UTF-8"?>
2 <beans xmlns="http://xmlns.jcp.org/xml/ns/javaee"
3     xmlns:xsi="http://www.w3.org/2001/XMLSchema-instance"
4     xsi:schemaLocation="http://xmlns.jcp.org/xml/ns/javaee
http://xmlns.jcp.org/xml/ns/javaee/beans_1_1.xsd"
5     bean-discovery-mode="all">
6 </beans>
```

Setting the bean discovery mode to all, as seen in Line 5, means that all classes will be discovered during scanning by the CDI container at application startup. So, whether a bean has a CDI annotation or not, as long as it's in the same archive (a bundle of a given Jakarta EE app), it will be discovered. This is what you will find in a lot of Jakarta EE code out there. It is also my preferred and recommended mode.

The CDI Container

The word *container* is most often associated with dependency injections. So what is the CDI container? It's the heartbeat of your CDI code. It validates your CDI code at application startup and ensures that all your CDI code is valid. It's very rare to get a CDI runtime error.

The CDI container is responsible for creating contextual instances of your beans, adding relevant CDI magic to those created instances, assigning them to relevant contexts, and finally destroying those instances when the contexts they're bound to get destroyed.

You can think of the CDI container as a black box that only appears to answer your requests and disappears into the shadows when not needed. You as a developer will mostly not need to think much about the CDI container, however. You just have to know it's there in the background, and ready to answer your requests.

CDI Beans vs. Contextual Instances

Up to this point, the book has used the term *beans* and *contextual instances* quite freely, without defining what they mean. So, what exactly is meant by beans?

The CDI spec defines beans as a source of contextual objects that define application state and/or logic. These objects are called contextual instances of the bean.[2] All that means is that a bean is the Java class that you, as a developer, write.

You implement your bean logic in Java code and then use relevant CDI annotations to provide it with attributes that you want the bean's contextual instance to posses. It is the template from which instances can be created and injected in the dependency injection process. The CDI container discovers your beans at application startup by scanning your application archive.

A bean then is just a collection of metadata associated with your Java code, from which the container creates objects to satisfy a given dependency injection request. That CDI created object from your bean is what is called a contextual instance.

The set of attributes that you can give your beans are Qualifiers, Scopes, Alternatives, and Name. These attributes are discussed throughout the rest of the book.

---

[2]http://docs.jboss.org/cdi/spec/2.0/cdi-spec.html#concepts

Creating and Using Beans

As stated earlier, a CDI bean is just a regular Java class with CDI metadata applied in the form of annotations. Take a look at the most basic CDI bean here.

```
1
2 public class TableService {
3
4     private final Collection<TableNum> assignedTables = new HashSet<>
5 ();
6
7     public boolean assignTable(TableNum tableNum) {
8         return assignedTables.add(tableNum);
9     }
10
11     public boolean checkTableAvailability(TableNum tableNum) {
12         return assignedTables.contains(tableNum);
13     }
14 }
```

This code shows a very boring plain old Java object, with no explicit CDI annotations, called TableService. This class is a valid CDI bean because the CDI discovery mode is set to all. This means you can request contextual instances of this bean from the CDI container, and it will honor your request. This bean, by default, has a scope called @Dependent, meaning it takes the scope of whatever bean it is injected into.

However, in the restaurant application, you need to have only one instance of the TableService responsible for checking the availability and assignment of tables to guests. In this case, you need to modify the bean—or template—from which the only-one-instance contextual instance will be created.

@ApplicationScoped

To make this modification, you need to use the @ApplicationScoped[3]
annotation to define a metadata on the bean.

```
1  @ApplicationScoped
2  public class TableService {
3
4      private final Collection<TableNum> assignedTables = new HashSet<>
5  ();
6
7      public boolean assignTable(TableNum tableNum) {
8          return assignedTables.add(tableNum);
9      }
10
11     public boolean checkTableAvailability(TableNum tableNum) {
12         return assignedTables.contains(tableNum);
13     }
14 }
```

This code shows the TableService class now bearing an explicit bean-
defining annotation called @ApplicationScoped. This annotation tells the
CDI container to put the contextual instance of this bean in a specific, well
defined scope, or context, called application.

Scopes, or contexts, are a way of telling the CDI container how you
want it to manage the lifecycle of your contextual instances. Instances you
request from the CDI container will be placed in relevant contexts that are
determined by either the explicit metadata you provide along with your
bean code, or one that the CDI container defaults to.

So, what does the application scope or context mean? It means that
for TableService, you only want to have one contextual instance for
the entire application. Every single request for a TableService from

---

[3]https://docs.jboss.org/cdi/api/2.0/javax/enterprise/context/
ApplicationScoped.html

the CDI container will be serviced with the same contextual instance. Think of @ApplicationScoped as a shared state contextual instance across the lifetime of the deployed application. You can think of an ApplicationScoped bean as a singleton if you are familiar with other DI frameworks like Spring.

The good thing about CDI scopes is that they are well defined. You can predict when an instance will be in existence and when it will be destroyed. You can use this knowledge to craft powerful dependency graphs in your application. So what are the other available scopes aside from @ApplicationScoped?

Other CDI Scopes
@RequestScoped[4]

This scope binds a contextual instance to a context that is created and destroyed for every request. In a typical HTTP environment, every HTTP request will result in the creation of a new contextual instance and its destruction at the end of the request. In a non-HTTP environment, a bean annotated with @RequestScoped will have its contextual instances always created and destroyed for every given request.

In the restaurant application, you could have a class that searches for orders and is bound to a JSF facelet page. This class typically should be RequestScoped so that you have different instances for each request for a search. You would want a clean slate for every search request.

---

[4]https://docs.jboss.org/cdi/api/2.0/javax/enterprise/context/ RequestScoped.html

```
1 @RequestScoped
2 @Named
3 public class SearchBean {
4
5     @Inject
6     private SearchService searchService;
7
8     private Collection<Order> orders;
9
10    public void search(String searchQuery) {
11        orders = searchService.searchOrders(searchQuery);
12    }
13
14    public Collection<Order> getOrders() {
15        return orders;
16    }
17 }
18
```

In this code, you have a class named SearchBean that is annotated with @RequestScoped on Line 1 and @Named on Line 2. This explicitly tells the CDI container to bind every instance of this bean to a scope called request. For every request for a contextual instance of this bean, a new instance will be created and put in a new scope. So multiple requests by a given user will result in new instances for each request.

This kind of bean is typically called a *backing bean,* or roughly a *controller.* The @Named annotation is a built-in qualifier[5] that makes this bean available to JSF pages through the expression language[6].

---

[5]Qualifiers are covered in Chapter 10.
[6]https://javaee.github.io/tutorial/jsf-el.html

@SessionScoped[7]

This scope binds instances of an annotated bean to a context that spans a given user session. Think of a session context as a guard that follows a user around an application as long as they are interacting with the application. The session scope is more or less the HTTP session for a given user.

In the restaurant application, you could have a bean that tracks a logged-in user, where that logged-in user could be the restaurant manager or cashier.

```
1 @SessionScoped
2 public class UserSession implements Serializable {
3
4     private String userName;
5     private LocalDateTime loggedInTime;
6     private LocalDateTime loggedOutTime;
7
8 }
```

In this code, you have a bean named UserSession that is annotated with @SessionScoped on Line 1. This tells the CDI container to create an instance of this class per user per session. So every user will have one contextual instance of this class for each session. Multiple requests for an instance of this class by a user in the same session will result in the same contextual instance being supplied.

---

[7]https://docs.jboss.org/cdi/api/2.0/javax/enterprise/context/
SessionScoped.html

Of note in this bean declaration is that it implements the Serializable interface, as shown on Line 2. This is good practice because the contextual instance might get passivated—or saved—by the container to save system resources when not in use. So it's good practice to mark it with the Serializable interface.

@ConversationScoped[8]

Conversation scoped beans are used to perform tasks that transcend one request but are shorter than a session. A typical example of @ConversationScoped use case is placing an order. Order items are held in a cart from the time a user starts picking items and are finally emptied when the user checks out. In between, the user might navigate across multiple pages of the application.

You can use conversation scoped beans to manage such a conversation between the user and your application without having to necessarily keep the bean alive once the user is done with the shopping.

Conversation scoped beans are by default in a transient state, that is, they're eligible to be destroyed at any time. Unlike the other scopes you've seen so far, you will have to initiate a bean into a conversation state manually. How do you do that? Back to the restaurant application, you could have a bean-annotated @ConversationScoped that is used to place an order in the system.

---

[8]https://docs.jboss.org/cdi/api/2.0/javax/enterprise/context/
ConversationScoped.html

```
 1 @ConversationScoped
 2 public class OrderService implements Serializable {
 3
 4     @Inject
 5     Conversation conversation;
 6
 7     public void beginOrderProcess() {
 8         if (conversation.isTransient()) {
 9             conversation.begin();
10         }
11     }
12
13     public void addItemsOrder() {
14
15     }
16
17     public void endOrderProcess() {
18         if (!conversation.isTransient()) {
19             conversation.end();
20         }
21     }
22 }
```

In this code, you have a bean called OrderService that is annotated @ConversationScoped on Line 1. This bean also bears the Serializable marker interface because it might get passivated by the container.

Line 4 uses the @Inject annotation to request a contextual object of a bean type called Conversation, on Line 5. This is the first time you are using the @Inject annotation. It's the magic wand for requesting contextual instances from the CDI container. The annotated bean type Conversation is a CDI bean that the container provides for you. It's not part of the developer code.

The Conversation bean has methods that you use to check if a bean is transient or not, begin and end conversations, and get the ID of the current conversation. Line 7 defines a method called beginOrderProcess() that first checks if the current instance is in transient mode. If it is, the begin() method is invoked on the injected Conversation instance.

Line 13 then defines a method called addItemsToOrder() that is responsible for adding items to the cart. This method can be implemented in any way depending on the issue at hand.

Line 17 finally declares a method called endConversation() that determines whether or not a bean is transient and proceeds to invoke the end() method on the injected Conversation object. Invoking the end() method makes the OrderService instance transient, ready to have its context destroyed.

Dependent Pseudo-Scope[9]

@Dependent is a pseudo-scope according to the CDI spec. It is the default scope a bean is scoped to when no explicit scopes are declared for it. Pseudo-scoped beans have at least two important points that distinguish them from other scopes:

- No injected instance of the bean is ever shared between multiple injection points.

- Any instance of the bean injected into an object that is being created by the container is bound to the lifecycle of the created object.

---

[9]https://docs.jboss.org/cdi/api/2.0/javax/enterprise/context/
Dependent.html

This implies that every request for a dependent scoped bean results in a new instance and the life of that instance is bound to the life of its injection point. Generally, I recommend that you explicitly declare scopes for your beans as an application developer.

So far you have seen the various contexts that are provided to you out-of-the-box by the CDI container. You have seen @ApplicationScoped, @RequestScoped, @SessionScoped, and @ConversationScoped. However, one question I have not answered at this point is where and how to make a request for contextual instances. You have seen how to create your own CDI beans, but how do you use them? How do you put the CDI container to your service?

CDI Injection Points

There are three main injection points where you can use the @Inject annotation to request contextual instances from the CDI container.

Field Injection Point

You saw your first injection point when you looked at the OrderService class earlier, reproduced here.

```
1 @ConversationScoped
2 public class OrderService implements Serializable {
3
4     @Inject
5     Conversation conversation;
6
7     public void beginOrderProcess() {
8         if (conversation.isTransient()) {
9             conversation.begin();
10        }
11    }
12
13    public void addItemsOrder() {
14
15    }
16
17    public void endOrderProcess() {
18        if (!conversation.isTransient()) {
19            conversation.end();
20        }
21    }
22 }
```

Line 4 uses the @Inject annotation on bean type Conversation. This
is a field injection point where you are requesting that the CDI container
create a contextual instance of the Conversation bean and inject it into the
provided variable of that type. Field injection is by far the most popular,
and in my view, most intuitive way of requesting dependencies.

Method Injection

Method injection is when a method is annotated with the @Inject
annotation with one or more parameters. These methods are called
initializer methods and will be invoked automatically by the container.
All parameters of a method injection point must be valid CDI beans.

Constructor Injection

Constructor injection is when you annotate a bean constructor with the
@Inject annotation with one or more parameters. All parameters will be
resolved by the container. Only one constructor injection is allowed per
CDI bean.

```
1  @RequestScoped
2  public class SearchService {
3
4      private final Collection<Order> searchResults = new HashSet<>();
5
6      QueryService queryService;
7
8      @Inject
9      public SearchService(QueryService qS) {
10         this.queryService = qS;
11     }
12
13     public Collection<Order> searchOrders(String reqQueryString, String... optionalQueryStrings) {
14         //perform search in datastore and put results in searchResults
15
16         return searchResults;
17     }
18 }
19
```

In the modified SearchService bean shown here, Line 6 declares a
field of type QueryService, which is itself a bean. Line 8 uses @Inject on
the constructor declaration (Line 9) to inject an instance of QueryService
into the parameter. You then use this injected parameter to initialize the
QueryService field declared in Line 6. There are other injection points as

well, found in producer methods and observer methods, and you will look at them a little later in this chapter.

Which is the best injection point?

Given the injection points supported by CDI, you might be wondering which is best. They are all good in different contexts. But as a rule of thumb, I always go with field injection. I find that it is easier to read and shows my intention right from the beginning of the code. But please feel free to choose what works best for your given project.

You now have seen CDI beans, the various scopes you can assign their contextual instances to, and the points that you can request for those contextual instances. CDI, however, has two broad kinds of beans. What you have looked at so far are called *managed beans*. The other kind of bean are *session beans,* not to be confused with session contexts.

Kinds of CDI Beans

Managed Beans

Managed beans are what you have seen so far in this book. They are Java classes that have either explicit CDI annotations for beans that have the bean-discovery-mode of the beans.xml file set to annotated, or implicit annotations for beans that have the bean-discovery-mode set to all. In addition, a bean is a managed bean if:

- It is not a non-static inner class.

- It is a concrete class or is annotated with @Decorator.

- It has an appropriate constructor, as one of the following:

  - The class has a constructor with no parameters

  - The class declares a constructor annotated with @Inject

For a given managed bean like the following:

```
1  @RequestScoped
2  public class SearchService {
3
4
5      private final Collection<Order> searchResults = new HashSet<>();
6      public Collection<Order> searchOrders(String reqQueryString, String... optionalQueryStrings) {
7          //perform search in datastore and put results in searchResults
8
9          return searchResults;
10     }
11 }
12
```

Its set of bean types includes:

- All super classes up to `java.lang.Object`

- All implemented interfaces, directly or indirectly

- The bean class itself

Session Beans

Session beans are Java classes annotated with metadata from the Enterprise JavaBeans[10] spec. Technically, local Stateless, Stateful, and Singleton EJBs are automatically CDI beans that support the various CDI services like injection, interception, and scoping. Using EJBs in a CDI application makes the features of both specs available to you.

---

[10]https://download.oracle.com/otndocs/jcp/ejb-3_2-fr-spec/index.html

Creating session bean is quite simple, as seen in the following code.

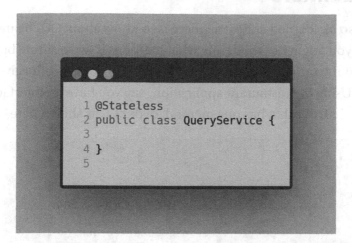

```
1 @Stateless
2 public class QueryService {
3
4 }
5
```

In this code, the QueryService class is annotated with @Stateless. This makes the bean both a CDI managed bean and a Stateless EJB. You can inject instances on this bean anywhere you can inject a managed bean. The EJB spec aims at making the development of a business component easy and almost effortless.

The @Stateless annotation on the QueryService transforms it into a class that has transactional methods by default. This class is pooled, secured, and has other helpful features that you would have had to worry about. Do take a look at the EJB spec for more information about the power of that API.

The bean type of a session bean includes:

- All super classes up to java.lang.Object

- All implemented interfaces, directly or indirectly (for beans with local interfaces)

- The bean class itself

CDI Qualifiers

You have so far learned almost all there is to know about CDI beans. However, you might be wondering what happens if two or more beans implement the same interface and you want to inject using the given interface. Using the restaurant application, say you have an interface of type GenericOrder that has one method, order(), as shown here.

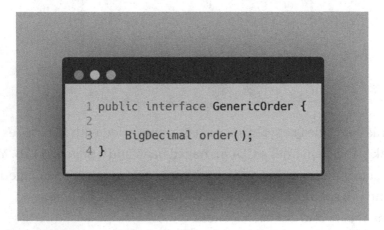

```
1 public interface GenericOrder {
2
3     BigDecimal order();
4 }
```

This interface has a method that returns the total of a given order. Say the restaurant has a website where a user can log on and place a self-service order to the kitchen for delivery. Patrons can also walk in and place orders that will be entered into the system by the restaurant attendants or cashiers.

You want to modify the @ConversationScoped OrderService bean to implement GenericOrder instead of having its own order method. This is shown in the following code.

```
1 @ConversationScoped
2 public class OrderService implements
3         GenericOrder, Serializable {
4
5     @Inject
6     Conversation conversation;
7
8     public void beginOrderProcess() {
9         if (conversation.isTransient()) {
10            conversation.begin();
11        }
12    }
13
14    @Override
15    public BigDecimal order() {
16        return null;
17    }
18
19    public void endOrderProcess() {
20        if (!conversation.isTransient()) {
21            conversation.end();
22        }
23    }
24
25
26 }
```

Line 15 implements the order() method of the GenericOrder interface. This OrderService will be used to service orders placed by patrons that physically walk into the restaurant to dine. You then need another service, called SelfService, that will implement GenericOrder to service the online clients.

The following code shows the SelfService implementation.

```
1 @ConversationScoped
2 public class SelfService implements
3        GenericOrder, Serializable {
4
5    @Inject
6    Conversation conversation;
7
8    public void beginOrderProcess() {
9        if (conversation.isTransient()) {
10            conversation.begin();
11        }
12    }
13
14    @Override
15    public BigDecimal order() {
16        return null;
17    }
18
19    public void endOrderProcess() {
20        if (!conversation.isTransient()) {
21            conversation.end();
22        }
23    }
24
25 }
```

The SelfService implementation is identical to the OrderService implementation, for now. You separate the two implementations now because in the future, clients who place their orders online will be treated completely differently, in terms of pricing, reward schemes, raffles, and other incentives that you will later introduce. So it's good practice to separate the two implementations now instead of having to refactor or introduce a new implementation after the application has become very complex.

So now you have two classes that implement the same interface. Trying to do an @Inject by the GenericOrder interface will fail, as shown here.

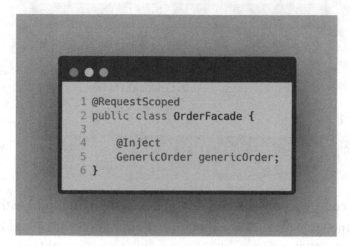

```
1  @RequestScoped
2  public class OrderFacade {
3
4      @Inject
5      GenericOrder genericOrder;
6  }
```

In this code, you have a CDI bean named OrderFacade that is request scoped. This bean has a field injection of type GenericOrder on Line 5. This code will compile fine but will fail deployment. The CDI container, remember, validates the archive to ensure you are in line with the requirements of the CDI spec.

This code will fail CDI container validation with a message that the injection point GenericOrder is ambiguous. This is because you have more than one class implementing the GenericOrder interface and are requesting a contextual instance through the interface. The container will not know which concrete bean type you want.

You will encounter these kinds of issues in your own code. To prevent these kinds of ambiguous dependency issues, the CDI spec gives you the concept of *qualifiers*. They are annotations that you create, place on beans that you want to identify with such annotations, and then annotate through injection points if you want injection points resolved to the annotated bean type. It sounds more complex than it is. Let's create two qualifiers for the order services—OnlineQualifier and InStoreQualifier.

```
1 @Qualifier
2 @Retention(RUNTIME)
3 @Target({FIELD, TYPE, METHOD, PARAMETER})
4 public @interface OnlineQualifier {
5
6 }
```

In this code, you have an annotation declaration on Line 4 with the name OnlineQualifier. This annotation is annotated with @Qualifier, which tells the CDI container that you want to have your OnlineQualifier annotation regarded as a CDI qualifier.

Lines 2 and 3 of the code set the retention and targets of the OnlineQualifier annotation. This is pretty much all you need to declare your annotation. You can use the same constructs for the InStoreQualifier as shown next.

```
1 @Qualifier
2 @Retention(RUNTIME)
3 @Target({FIELD, TYPE, METHOD, PARAMETER})
4 public @interface InStoreQualifier {
5
6 }
7
```

So, with these annotations declared, you now need to associate them with the respective beans you want to use them for. You use the OnlineQualifier to qualify the SelfService bean and the InStoreQualifier for the OrderService beans. The respective code samples are reproduced next.

```
1 @ConversationScoped
2 @OnlineQualifier
3 public class SelfService implements
4         GenericOrder, Serializable {
5
6     @Inject
7     Conversation conversation;
8
9     public void beginOrderProcess() {
10         if (conversation.isTransient()) {
11             conversation.begin();
12         }
13     }
14
15     @Override
16     public BigDecimal order() {
17         return null;
18     }
19
20     public void endOrderProcess() {
21         if (!conversation.isTransient()) {
22             conversation.end();
23         }
24     }
25
26 }
```

The OnlineQualifier is associated with the SelfService bean on Line 2 of the previous code.

```
1 @ConversationScoped
2 @InStoreQualifier
3 public class OrderService implements
4         GenericOrder, Serializable {
5
6     @Inject
7     Conversation conversation;
8
9     public void beginOrderProcess() {
10         if (conversation.isTransient()) {
11             conversation.begin();
12         }
13     }
14
15     @Override
16     public BigDecimal order() {
17         return null;
18     }
19
20     public void endOrderProcess() {
21         if (!conversation.isTransient()) {
22             conversation.end();
23         }
24     }
25 }
```

The InStoreQualifier is now associated with the OrderService bean on Line 2. So now you have two beans of the type GenericOrder, but with separate qualifiers. With this in place, you can now go back to the OrderFacade bean and qualify the GenericOrder injection point.

```
1 @RequestScoped
2 public class OrderFacade {
3     @Inject
4     @InStoreQualifier
5     GenericOrder genericOrder;
6 }
7
```

Line 4 uses the @InStoreQualifier to tell the container to resolve the GenericOrder type to the OrderService concrete type. This way, even though you request instances through a common interface implemented by more than one class, there is no ambiguity with regards to type resolution.

You can, in the same class, inject another GenericOrder field and qualify it with the OnlineQualifier, as shown next.

```
 1 @RequestScoped
 2 public class OrderFacade {
 3     @Inject
 4     @InStoreQualifier
 5     GenericOrder genericOrder;
 6
 7     @Inject
 8     @OnlineQualifier
 9     GenericOrder onlineOrder;
10 }
```

As you can see, there are two field injection points in the `OrderFace` bean now, both using the `GenericOrder` interface yet both qualified with their respective concrete type qualifiers.

This is how you can use qualifiers to prevent ambiguity in your code, while simultaneously improving the readability and extensibility of it. Qualifiers can be used for much more powerful tasks, though, as you will see in the "Events" section of this chapter.

Built-in Qualifiers

Aside from the ability to create your own CDI qualifiers, the CDI API also comes with some built-in qualifiers out-of-the-box. These are as follows:

- `@Any`[11]: This is a qualifier added to all beans by default, even if the bean does not declare any qualifiers.

- `@Named`[12]: This is a string based qualifier used to make instances of the annotated bean available for reference in a weakly typed environment, like a JSF page or JavaScript. It is also the most used annotation.

- `@Default`[13]: This qualifier is used automatically when a bean does not explicitly declare a qualify aside from `@Named`.

---

[11]https://docs.jboss.org/cdi/api/2.0/javax/enterprise/inject/Any.html

[12]https://docs.oracle.com/javaee/7/api/javax/inject/Named.html

[13]https://docs.jboss.org/cdi/api/2.0/javax/enterprise/inject/Default.html

- @Initialized[14]: This qualifier is used to qualify an automatically fired event when a context is initialized and ready to use. You will learn about events later in this chapter.

- @Destroyed[15]: This qualifier is used to qualify an automatically fired event when a context is destroyed.

Up to this point, you have learned quite a lot of CDI stuff, enough to make you capable of writing better. However, there's even more to learn, so let's take a look at the concept of CDI producers, what they are, and how you can use them.

CDI Producers

Producers in CDI are an API construct that you can use to turn beans or classes you don't own into CDI managed beans, complete with qualifiers and scopes. Back to the restaurant app, say you want to have the username of the currently executing user at any time. There are two ways you can achieve that.

The first is to simply @Inject the UserSession bean and invoke the getUserName() method on the instance. The second, more extensible, way is to create a producer method of type String that returns the username. This way, you can @Inject into a field of type String and the container will know where to get what you want. You can sweeten things by qualifying your producer methods.

---

[14]https://docs.jboss.org/cdi/api/2.0/javax/enterprise/context/
Initialized.html

[15]https://docs.jboss.org/cdi/api/2.0/javax/enterprise/context/
Destroyed.html

Method Producers

It is more simple than words make it, so let's look at the first producer method that returns the currently executing username.

```
 1 public class MyProducer {
 2
 3     @Inject
 4     UserSession userSession;
 5
 6     @Produces
 7     public String produceUserName() {
 8         return userSession.getUserName();
 9     }
10 }
```

In this code, you have a bean named MyProducer (for lack of imagination on my part that has an injected field of type UserSession on Line 4. Line 7 declares a method called produceUserName() that returns a String type. This method is annotated with @Produces[16] on Line 6. This annotation transforms this method into a CDI producer that will be consulted for instances to satisfy String injection types.

You can then use the producer method to inject String types into your other components, as shown here.

---

[16]https://docs.jboss.org/cdi/api/2.0/javax/enterprise/inject/Produces.html

```
1  @RequestScoped
2  public class OrderFacade {
3
4      @Inject
5      String userName;
6
7      @Inject
8      @InStoreQualifier
9      GenericOrder genericOrder;
10
11     @Inject
12     @OnlineQualifier
13     GenericOrder onlineOrder;
14 }
```

Line 4 uses @Inject to request an instance of type String into the userName field (Line 5) of the OrderFacade bean. This should work fine, assuming you do not use any third-party code in your application.

If you do, however, libraries such as OmniFaces[17] have producer methods that return String. In the restaurant app, you have the OmniFaces library as part of the application dependencies. So, the String injection point will cause the code to fail container validation at application startup, even though it will compile just fine.

---

[17]http://omnifaces.org/

In this case, you can use a qualifier to qualify the producer method and injection point. Take a look at the qualifier declaration here:

```
1 @Qualifier
2 @Retention(RUNTIME)
3 @Target({FIELD, TYPE, METHOD, PARAMETER})
4 public @interface UserNameQualifier {
5
6 }
7
```

In the previous code, you declare a qualifier called UserNameQualifier, which you associate with the producer method, as shown next.

```
 1 public class MyProducer {
 2
 3     @Inject
 4     UserSession userSession;
 5
 6     @Produces
 7     @UserNameQualifier
 8     public String produceUserName() {
 9         return userSession.getUserName();
10     }
11 }
```

Line 7 annotates the produceUserName() method with the @UserNameQualifier to ensure that you can distinguish this producer method from any other, whether in your own code or any third-party library. Finally, you qualify the injection point with the same qualifier.

```
 1 @RequestScoped
 2 public class OrderFacade {
 3
 4     @Inject
 5     @UserNameQualifier
 6     String userName;
 7
 8     @Inject
 9     @InStoreQualifier
10     GenericOrder genericOrder;
11
12     @Inject
13     @OnlineQualifier
14     GenericOrder onlineOrder;
15 }
16
```

Line 5 annotates the userName field with @UserNameQualifier to tell the container to consult the annotated producer field for instance to satisfy this injection point. This is how you can use producers methods in a nutshell.

What you have seen so far are producer methods. You could scope the producer method return type to a specific scope instead of leaving it to the default @Dependent scope. But, there is a caveat. According to the CDI API, "if a producer method sometimes returns a null value, or if a producer field sometimes contains a null value when accessed, then the producer method or field must have scope @Dependent."

You could have a situation where your code requests a userName when no user is logged in. In such a case, your producer method might return null, and thus you leave it to the default @Dependent scope. However, just know that you can annotate your producer methods with a specific scope and returned types from the method will be put in that context.

Producer Fields

Producer fields are similar to producer methods in that they both act as sources for contextual instances. Producer fields, however, are just fields of a bean annotated with the @Produces annotation. The annotated field can be equally qualified and scoped as can be done with a producer method. A typical use of producer fields is producing EntityManager[18] objects for JPA, as shown next.

```
1 public class MyProducer {
2
3     @Produces
4     @PersistenceContext
5     EntityManager entityManager;
6
7 }
8
```

Line 5 declares a field of type EntityManager, annotated with @PersistenceContext on Line 4 and @Produces on Line 3. This is a classic case of field producers where you are using two annotations from two APIs to produce an object. The @PersistenceContext annotation is from the JPA and is used to link this EntityManager object to the persistence

---

[18]https://docs.oracle.com/javaee/7/api/javax/persistence/
EntityManager.html

context. You then use the CDI @Produces annotation to make this field capable of satisfying the JPA EntityManager injection points in your code.

CDI Bean Lifecycle Callbacks

CDI beans, as has been discussed to this point, are managed by the container. All you have to do is request instances from the container. However, there are times when you'll need to do some for initialization, or de-initialization of your beans before you use them.

A typical example could be when you need to fetch some form of list from the database for display in the UI before the UI accesses the bean. Another example is releasing system resources held in a bean before the bean is destroyed. You will encounter these a lot in your own applications.

The CDI API gives you annotations you can place on methods to transform those methods into automatically invoked lifecycle callbacks.

@PostConstruct[19]

A method annotated @PostConstruct will be automatically invoked when a bean instance is fully constructed and all dependencies of the bean have been satisfied, but just before the bean is put into service.

A method annotated @PostConstruct must not have a return type nor take any parameters, except for interceptors (you'll learn about them later), for which case they can take an InvocationContext[20] object. A @PostConstruct annotated method can be private, package private, protected, or public.

---

[19]https://docs.oracle.com/javaee/7/api/javax/annotation/PostConstruct.html

[20]https://docs.oracle.com/javaee/7/api/javax/interceptor/InvocationContext.html

In this code, you want to pre-populate a list with the last 10 orders of a self-service user that logs on to use the online portal. In the SelfService bean, as shown here, you can use the @PostConstruct callback method.

```
1 @ConversationScoped
2 @OnlineQualifier
3 public class SelfService implements
4         GenericOrder, Serializable {
5
6     List<Order> lastOrders = new ArrayList<>();
7
8     @PostConstruct
9     private void init() {
10          //Populate list from DB
11     }
12
13 }
```

Line 6 declares a Order typed List object. Line 8 declares the init() method on Line 9 as a callback method with the @PostConstruct annotation. The method signature is straightforward—it returns void, is named init (part of my naming convention), and is declared private. At runtime, the container will automatically invoke this method once all injection points in the bean have been satisfied but just before the bean is put into service.

@PreDestroy[21]

This annotation can be used on a method that should be invoked just before a bean instance is destroyed by the container.

So far you've seen how all the of the various CDI API constructs work together. Next up, you'll learn about the concept of CDI interceptors, what they are, what problem they solve, and how you can create them.

CDI Interceptors

For every application, you will have situations where you need to dynamically perform tasks on bean invocations that are orthogonal to the core function of those beans. CDI interceptors are similar in nature to Aspect Oriented Programming as used in the Spring Framework. A typical example is logging and security.

In your code, for example, you would want to log method invocations on certain beans. You could manually implement the logging feature in all the beans you want to log method invocations on. However, that would be implementing features in the beans that aren't really their core. Also, because the logging feature is a cross-cutting concern, you should abstract that away from the beans. CDI interceptors can help you achieve that goal.

There are two parts to realizing interceptors using the CDI API. The first is to create an interceptor-binding annotation. The second is to link the interceptor-binding annotation to a bean that will implement the interceptor method. Let's first create an interceptor-binding annotation in the restaurant app.

---

[21]https://docs.oracle.com/javaee/7/api/javax/annotation/PreDestroy.
html

```
1 @Inherited
2 @Target({TYPE, METHOD})
3 @Retention(RUNTIME)
4 @InterceptorBinding
5 public @interface Logging {
6
7 }
8
```

Line 5 declares an annotation with the name Logging. You could name your interceptor-binding annotation anything. Line 4 uses the @InterceptorBinding[22] annotation to declare that this annotation is an interceptor-binding annotation. Note the target of the annotation is Type and Method, meaning that you can use this interceptor for a whole class or just a method of that class. The @InterceptorBinding annotation is from the javax.interceptor package. Now let's implement the bean that will carry out the logic of the interceptor.

```
1  @Interceptor
2  @Logging
3  @Priority(Interceptor.Priority.APPLICATION)
4  public class LoggingBean {
5
6      @Inject
7      private Logger logger;
8
9      @AroundInvoke
10     public Object log(InvocationContext invocationContext) throws Exception {
11
12         //Log the invocation using whatever logging framework. We'll just use java.util.Logger
13         logger.log(Level.INFO, "Method " + invocationContext.getMethod().getName() + " invoked.");
14         return invocationContext.proceed();
15     }
16 }
```

----

[22]https://docs.oracle.com/javaee/7/api/javax/interceptor/
InterceptorBinding.html

Line 4 declares a class called LoggingBean annotated with @Interceptor on Line 1. This annotation makes this class an interceptor bean. Line 2 annotates the same class with the @Logging interceptor annotation. This links the annotation to this class. This means anytime you annotate a method or class with the @Logging annotation, the CDI container will instantiate this class to carry the logic of the interceptor.

Line 3 also annotates the class with the @Priority annotation, taking a Interceptor.Priority.APPLICATION as a parameter. Before Java EE 7, you needed to activate interceptors through an XML config file. However, after version 7, you could use the @Priority annotation to activate and order/prioritize your interceptors. In this case, you are passing it the APPLICATION constant, which is just an int value.

Line 10 declares a method called log() that takes a single object of type InvocationContext[23], returns Object, and throws Exception. This method is annotated with @AroundInvoke on Line 9. The log() method is the place you implement the logic of the interceptor, using an injected logger—Lines 6 and 7—to log the invoked method name. In this method, you can implement any logic that cuts across classes.

The InvocationContext object is a bean that gives you information about the—drumroll—context of the invocation for which this interceptor has been dispatched. It has methods you can use to get information about the method parameter if the interceptor was dispatched for a method, information about the constructor if this interceptor was dispatched for a class, get and set method parameters, and a method to tell the container to proceed with the invocation of the next interceptor, or method if none.

Line 14 invokes the proceed() method on the InvocationContext. This tells the container to proceed to the next interceptor if more than one has been dispatched, or to the method call if this is the only interceptor.

---

[23]https://docs.oracle.com/javaee/7/api/javax/interceptor/
InvocationContext.html

Assuming you were implementing security instead of logging, and after doing some security checks, your code decides the currently executing user should not be invoking the target method for which this interceptor was dispatched, you can return null and the container will not proceed to invoke the target method.

With your interceptor implemented, all you have to do to use it is annotate a method you want to log in a given bean. Now you can log method order invocations on your OrderService bean.

```
1 @ConversationScoped
2 @InStoreQualifier
3 public class OrderService implements
4         GenericOrder, Serializable {
5
6     @Inject
7     Conversation conversation;
8
9     public void beginOrderProcess() {
10            if (conversation.isTransient()) {
11                conversation.begin();
12            }
13    }
14
15    @Override
16    @Logging
17    public BigDecimal order() {
18            return null;
19    }
20
21    public void endOrderProcess() {
22            if (!conversation.isTransient()) {
23                conversation.end();
24            }
25    }
26 }
```

Line 16 uses the @Logging annotation to log invocations of the order()
method on the OrderService bean. Every invocation of this method will
cause the container to dispatch the interceptor. And since you ask for the
invocation to proceed at the end of the interceptor logic implementation,
the invocation will proceed to the order() method after logging.

This is how simple it is to implement interceptors using the CDI
API. You create your interceptor-binding annotation, then link that
annotation to an interceptor bean with a method annotated with
@AroundInvoke that implements your interceptor logic. To use your
interceptor, you annotate any method or class—depending on your
interceptor annotation target—with your interceptor annotation. Next up,
you'll learn about CDI events, what they are, why you'd want to use them,
how to create them, and how to use them. Let's go.

CDI Events

Synchronous Events

A CDI event is an API construct that helps your application components
communicate with each other without any form of compile-time
dependencies, or without them even knowing about each other. It entails
an event object of any valid Java type, optionally with qualifiers and one or
more event listeners, also optionally with qualifiers.

The Event[24] object fires an event of its payload type, and the CDI
container automatically invokes observers that are observing that
particular event fired based on the event payload type and, optionally,
qualifiers. In the restaurant application, say you want to have feature where
you send an SMS to a user who places an order online to acknowledge
receipt of their order and to give them an ETA.

---

[24]https://docs.jboss.org/cdi/api/2.0/javax/enterprise/event/Event.html

You could implement such a feature using events. First, you need an Event object with a suitable payload and an observer that observes that same payload event type. Here that is in code.

```
1 @ConversationScoped
2 @OnlineQualifier
3 public class SelfService implements
4         GenericOrder, Serializable {
5
6     @Inject
7     Event<ApplicationUser> messageEvent;
8
9     @Inject
10    UserSession userSession;
11
12    @Override
13    public BigDecimal order() {
14        //fire a message event to send SMS before returning from this method
15        messageEvent.fire(userSession.getCurrentUser());
16        return null;
17    }
18
19
20 }
21
```

You start by using @Inject to request an Event bean typed to ApplicationUser on Line 7. The event interface is the starting point of the CDI event mechanism. The injected Event instance is then used to fire an ApplicationUser event in the order() method on Line 15, using the fire(T event) method.

Because the Event bean is typed to an ApplicationUser object (Line 7), the fire method used to fire the event must be passed an instance of the ApplicationUser class. This is the event payload, or data that will be passed to event observers, and in this case, it's also used to choose which observers to invoke for the event. You use the injected UserSession—Lines 9 and 10—in the SelfService class to get the currently executing user by invoking the getCurrentUser() method (Line 15).

The ApplicationUser class is a bean that models an application user, as shown here.

```
1 public class ApplicationUser {
2
3        private String userName;
4        private String email;
5        private String address;
6        private String mobileNumber;
7        private String hashedPassword;
8 }
9
```

The updated UserSession bean is shown next.

```
1 @SessionScoped
2 public class UserSession implements Serializable {
3
4        private LocalDateTime loggedInTime;
5        private LocalDateTime loggedOutTime;
6
7        private ApplicationUser currentUser;
8
9        public ApplicationUser getCurrentUser() {
10               return currentUser;
11        }
12
13
14 }
15
```

The UserSession bean now has a field of type ApplicationUser on Line 7. This is going to be set in one way or another by some kind of security layer, after a user successfully authenticates herself to the system. For now, you'll just use it as it is.

With the event fired, you need at least one observer to listen for that particular event. Because this event has no explicit qualifiers, the event observer will be selected based on the event payload type for which it is observing. Here is the observer code.

```
1 public class MyEventListener {
2
3     void smsObserver(@Observes ApplicationUser applicationUser) {
4         try {
5             Thread.sleep(5000);
6             //Simulate sending SMS, which might be a long running task
7         } catch (InterruptedException e) {
8             e.printStackTrace();
9         }
10    }
11 }
12
```

The event observer is declared in a bean class of type MyEventListener. It has one method called smsObserver that takes one argument of type ApplicationUser. The only new CDI API in this method is the @Observes annotation. This annotation transforms this method into a CDI observer for event type ApplicationUser, as fired from the SelfService class.

At runtime, when an event is fired from the SelfService class, the container will cycle through all the event observers looking for events that observe the specific type fired. Once it comes across this method, it will invoke it and pass in the payload passed to the fire method of the event object.

In the observer, you simulate a long-running task of sending an SMS, which might take sometime because it has to do with network communication. Once the method returns, execution is returned to the point of fire and then continues on from there.

There are a few rules to declare an event observer:

- The return type must be void.

- It must have at least one parameter annotated with @Observes for the event type to be observed.

- Other parameters to the observer method must be CDI managed beans capable of injection.

- The observer must be declared in a CDI bean.

As shown, firing and observing events with CDI is very easy and intuitive. As you might have noticed, the event observer has nothing to do with the SelfService class. The MyEventListener bean is oblivious of any bean that fires an event. You can have multiple event firing points for the same event type and each time your event observer will be invoked, without all components knowing about each other. This is compelling if you think about it.

Async Events

You can, however, improve this event mechanism in the restaurant application code. If you notice, the event observer in the MyEventListener class performs a blocking task. You might want to improve the responsiveness of this application by spawning long-running tasks to new threads. So instead of sending an SMS in the same thread that fired the event, you could do that in a different thread. Can you do that with the event mechanism of CDI? Yes of course. Here's how, starting from the event-firing side.

```
1 @ConversationScoped
2 @OnlineQualifier
3 public class SelfService implements
4         GenericOrder, Serializable {
5
6     @Inject
7     Event<ApplicationUser> messageEvent;
8
9     @Override
10    public BigDecimal order() {
11
12        //fire a message event to send SMS before returning from this method
13 //       messageEvent.fire(userSession.getCurrentUser());
14        messageEvent.fireAsync(userSession.getCurrentUser());
15        return null;
16    }
17
18 }
```

In this code, you use the same injected `Event` object—Lines 7 and 8—to fire an `ApplicationUser` event on Line 14. The difference, however, is that you invoked the `fireAsync` method instead of the plain fire. This method fires an asynchronous event for all async observers to listen for it. Async events return control immediately. The observer method is executed simultaneously, or asynchronously. Here's the async event observer implementation.

```
1 public class MyEventListener {
2
3     void smsAsyncObserver(@ObservesAsync ApplicationUser applicationUser) {
4         try {
5             Thread.sleep(5000);
6             //Simulate sending SMS, which might be a long running task
7             //You get the user phone number from ApplicationUser#getMobileNumber()
8
9         } catch (InterruptedException e) {
10             e.printStackTrace();
11         }
12     }
13 }
```

Line 3 declares a method, `smsAsyncObserver`, that takes an `ApplicationUser` object as a parameter. The only new thing is the annotation you use for the parameter. Instead of `@Observes` as earlier, the code uses `@ObservesAsync`. This is how you create an observer to listen to async events.

Because this code has only one async firing point and one async observer of the same payload type, this observer will be invoked. The best thing is that this observer will not block. Once it's invoked, execution will return to the `order()` method in the `SelfService` bean. This way, you can conveniently send the SMS without affecting the responsiveness of the application. This is how you implement async events in CDI. But there's more.

You can use qualifiers to fire and observe events of the same type, but for different purposes. You can qualify the event object at the injection point and the observer at the declaration point. The container will then link the observer to the event based on the qualifier. It is effortless to implement.

Qualifying Events

Let's say in your application, you decide to send an SMS to all clients, whether self-service or in-person diners. However, you want to have different message content for the two classes of clients. To do that, you need to qualify your events and observers with requisite qualifiers.

```
 1 @ConversationScoped
 2 @OnlineQualifier
 3 public class SelfService implements
 4         GenericOrder, Serializable {
 5
 6     @Inject
 7     @OnlineQualifier
 8     Event<ApplicationUser> messageEvent;
 9
10     @Override
11     public BigDecimal order() {
12
13         //fire a message event to send SMS before returning from this method
14 //        messageEvent.fire(userSession.getCurrentUser());
15         messageEvent.fireAsync(userSession.getCurrentUser());
16         return null;
17     }
18 }
19
```

This code has only one change. On Line 7, you use `@OnlineQualifier` to qualify the injected event object. This marks this event as qualified and will only be listened to by observers with the same qualifier. Here's the observer.

```
1 public class MyEventListener {
2
3     void smsAsyncObserver(@ObservesAsync @OnlineQualifier ApplicationUser applicationUser) {
4         try {
5             Thread.sleep(5000);
6             //Simulate sending SMS, which might be a long running task
7             //You get the user phone number from ApplicationUser#getMobileNumber()
8
9         } catch (InterruptedException e) {
10            e.printStackTrace();
11        }
12    }
13 }
14
```

The `async` observer is the same as before except for the method parameter on Line 3, where you annotate the `ApplicationUser` with `@OnlineQualifier`. This single annotation links this observer to the event in `SelfService`. You can now fire an async event in the `SelfService` class and have this observer invoked. However, all of this is quite useless if you have just one event-firing point and one observer. The power of qualifying events comes in to play when you have more than one event. Take a look at that scenario.

```
1 @ConversationScoped
2 @InStoreQualifier
3 public class OrderService implements
4         GenericOrder, Serializable {
5
6     @Inject
7     @InStoreQualifier
8     Event<ApplicationUser> messageEvent;
9
10    @Inject
11    UserSession userSession;
12
13
14    @Override
15    @Logging
16    public BigDecimal order() {
17
18        messageEvent.fireAsync(userSession.getCurrentUser());
19        return null;
20    }
21 }
22
```

This code shows the OrderService bean with two new fields—Event and UserSession. The event object on Line 8 is qualified with the @InStoreQualifier on Line 7. You then fire an async event on Line 18 after an order is placed by a diner. This fired event can only be observed by @InStoreQualifier qualified observers, as follows.

```
1 public class MyEventListener {
2
3     void smsInStore(@ObservesAsync @InStoreQualifier ApplicationUser applicationUser) {
4         try {
5             Thread.sleep(5000);
6             //Simulate sending SMS, which might be a long running task
7             //You get the user phone number from ApplicationUser#getMobileNumber()
8
9         } catch (InterruptedException e) {
10            e.printStackTrace();
11        }
12    }
13 }
14
```

In this code, you declare an observer on Line 3 called smsInStore with one parameter type—ApplicationUser. This parameter is annotated with @ObservesAsynch and @InStoreQualifier, effectively making this observer responsible for the event fired from the OrderService class. This is how you can combine the various CDI API constructs to create very powerful applications, all the while keeping your code easy to read and maintainable.

Transactional Event Observers

All the event observers will be called when the event is fired. There are times, however, when you need an event observer to be called at a specific time during a transaction. As an example, say you have an ApplicationUser class in your application. You would like to send a welcome email to a self-service user who successfully registers with the application. However, you want to send the email only if the user is successfully persisted in your datastore, or more technically, when the transaction completes successfully.

To do that, you create a new qualifier, CreateUserQualifier, fire an event, and declare a transactional observer that gets called only if the transaction completes successfully. The code starts with the qualifier.

```
1 @Qualifier
2 @Retention(RUNTIME)
3 @Target({FIELD, TYPE, METHOD, PARAMETER})
4 public @interface CreateUserQualifier {
5
6 }
7
```

Line 4 shows an annotation declaration called `CreateUserQualifier`, with the requisite qualifier metadata declared on Lines 1-3.

```
1 @Stateless
2 public class PersistenceService {
3
4     @Inject
5     @CreateUserQualifier
6     Event<ApplicationUser> emailEvent;
7
8     public ApplicationUser persistUser(ApplicationUser applicationUser) {
9         //Persist new user into datastore, returning the persisted user.
10        emailEvent.fire(applicationUser);
11
12        return applicationUser;
13
14    }
15 }
```

Line 2 of this code declares the `PersistenceService` bean, which is set as a stateless EJB (Line 1). You inject an event object on Line 6, which is qualified on Line 5 with `@CreateUserQualifier`. The class then declares a method called `persistUser` on Line 8 that takes an `ApplicationUser` object as the parameter. In this method, you would store the user in the datastore using some form of data API. You then fire an event on Line 10 with the `ApplicationUser` object as the payload.

Because the `persistUser` method is declared in an EJB, it will be executed in a transactional context. So you know that the event is being fired in a transactional context. Now you can examine the observer for this event.

```
1 public class MyEventListener {
2
3     void sendEmail(@Observes(during = TransactionPhase.AFTER_SUCCESS)
4                    @CreateUserQualifier ApplicationUser applicationUser) {
5         //Send email using MessagingService
6     }
7 }
8
```

Line 3 declares an observer called sendEmail that takes an ApplicationUser as the payload. It is qualified with @CreateUserQualifier and annotated with @Observes. This time, however, the @Observes annotation has a value set for the during parameter. The value of the during field of the @Observes annotation can be set to any of the following:

- TransactionPhase.IN_PROGRESS: The event observer is invoked when the event is fired, without regard to the transaction phase. This is the default value for all the @Observes you have seen so far.

- TransactionPhase.BEFORE_COMPLETION: The event observer is called during the before completion phase of the transaction.

- TransactionPhase.AFTER_COMPLETION: The event observer is called during the after completion phase of the transaction.

- TransactionPhase.AFTER_FAILURE: The event observer is called during the after completion phase of the transaction, but only if the transaction failed.

- TransactionPhase.AFTER_SUCCESS: The event observer is called during the after completion phase of the transaction, but only if the transaction completed successfully.

The last value was used in the observer declaration. What you want is for this observer to be invoked only if the transaction in which you are persisting the new user completes successfully, in which case you know for certain the user has been persisted in the datastore. There is no point in sending a welcome email to a user who has not successfully registered.

CHAPTER 9

CDI Stereotypes

CDI stereotypes are an API construct that help you group together similar architectural patterns into one annotation. In the restaurant application you learned about in Chapter 8, there is a class named QueryService that you need to transform into a transactional, logged, request scoped bean to carry out a query service in the data layer.

Now assume this requirement will apply to other beans as well. What this means is that QueryService would look like the following.

```
1 @RequestScoped
2 @Transactional
3 @Logging
4 public class QueryService {
5
6     @Inject
7     private EntityManager entityManager;
8 }
```

Lines 1-3 use the @RequestScoped, @Transactional, and @Logging annotations to declare the QueryService bean. The @Transactional annotation is an interceptor from the Java Transaction API. @Loggin is the logging interceptor. If the application grows and there is a need for more service layer classes, every single one of those classes is going to have to repeat these annotations.

© Luqman Saeed 2020
L. Saeed, *Introducing Jakarta EE CDI*, https://doi.org/10.1007/978-1-4842-5642-8_9

Using CDI stereotypes, you can group these commonly required annotations into one annotation so that using that single stereotype will result in the activation of all the other annotations. You can declare a CDIService stereotype to use on the QueryService class as follows.

```
1 @Stereotype
2 @RequestScoped
3 @Transactional
4 @Logging
5 @Named
6 @Retention(RUNTIME)
7 @Target(TYPE)
8 public @interface CDIService {
9 }
```

This code snippet declares a stereotype called CDIService using the @Stereotype annotation on Line 1. Line 2 then declares this stereotype as having a request scope. Line 3 declares CDIService as being @Transactional, meaning that every method in a class annotated with @CDIService will be run as a transaction. Line 4 declares @Logging, making @CDIService loggable. Line 5 then uses the CDI qualifier called @Named to make any @CDIService annotated class available to any JSF page. Line 6 declares the retention as RUNTIME and Line 7 declares the target as TYPE, meaning that @CDIService can only be used on classes.

Now you can apply this newly created stereotype to the QueryService bean to make it instantly a request-scoped, transactional, loggable, named bean.

```
1 @CDIService
2 public class QueryService {
3
4 }
```

Line 1 in this code snippet shows the use of the @CDIService stereotype on the QueryService. So with that, you have replaced the need for (and the tedious repetition of) four annotations with just one.

This is how you can use CDI stereotypes to simplify and compact your code. If you need to make your data layer service classes application instead of request scope, all you have to do is change the scope at the stereotype definition level and that will instantly be available on all @CDIService annotated beans.

CHAPTER 10

The CDI Ecosystem

The Contexts and Dependency Injection (CDI) API is at the heart of the entire Jakarta EE platform. CDI provides a powerful Service Provider Interface (SPI) that allows third-party libraries to create portable extensions for the platform. In effect, CDI makes it easy for other projects to integrate into Jakarta EE.

A portable extension may integrate into the platform by

- Providing its beans, interceptors, and decorators to the container

- Injecting dependencies into its objects using the dependency injection service

- Providing a context implementation for a custom scope

- Augmenting or overriding the annotation-based metadata with metadata from some other source

The two notable CDI extensions are the Apache Delta Spike[1] and Eclipse MicroProfile[2] projects.

---

[1]https://deltaspike.apache.org/
[2]https://microprofile.io/

© Luqman Saeed 2020
L. Saeed, *Introducing Jakarta EE CDI*, https://doi.org/10.1007/978-1-4842-5642-8_10

Eclipse MicroProfile

Eclipse MicroProfile is an Eclipse Foundation-led project aimed at making the Jakarta EE platform a cloud-native enterprise development choice. It features a number of APIs that together form a powerful toolset for creating resilient, portable enterprise Java applications.

The most obvious CDI extension from MicroProfile is the Config API. The MP Config API aims at simplifying application configuration in different environments and from different sources without the need to redeploy or restart the application.

An application might need different port numbers for different requests, or certain features need to be switched on or off based on certain configurations. The Config API aims at externalizing application configuration so that changes can be made without having to restart/redeploy your code.

To get started with MicroProfile, you need to add the dependency to your project, as shown here. Almost all the Jakarta EE app servers support MP.

```
1 <dependency>
2       <groupId>org.eclipse.microprofile</groupId>
3       <artifactId>microprofile</artifactId>
4       <version>3.2</version>
5       <type>pom</type>
6       <scope>provided</scope>
7 </dependency>
```

This code snippet adds the latest MicroProfile API to your project dependencies, giving you access to the entire suite of sub-projects. For example, assume that in the restaurant app, in the SelfService.java class, you need a configurable string that contains a welcome message for self-serve customers.

To achieve this, you first need to create at least one config source—a place to get values from—in the app. The following code snippet shows the `microprofile-config.properties` file, located in the META-INF folder.

```
1 self-service=Welcome to Awesome Restaurant Self Service
```

This code snippet shows a key, called `self-service`, that has a string value. To use this in your code, you simply create a `String` field and inject this value into it using a qualifier from the MicroProfile Config API, as shown here.

```
1     @Inject
2     @ConfigProperty(name = "self-service")
3     private String selfServiceWelcome;
```

Line 1 of this code snippet uses the `@Inject` annotation in combination with `@ConfigProperty` on Line 2 to inject the value of the field defined in the properties file. `@ConfigProperty` is a MicroProfile Config Qualifier that takes two parameters—name is the key of the config value you want and a default value in the absence of a value in any of the config sources.

In this code, you set the name of the `@ConfigProperty` annotation to the key of the `self-service` string. You could as well have defined a default value, as shown next, to be injected into the `selfServiceWelcome` field in the absence of a value in the properties file or any other config source.

```
1     @Inject
2     @ConfigProperty(name = "self-service", defaultValue = "Hello, and welcome!")
3     private String selfServiceWelcome;
4
```

From this code snippet, in the absence of a value, the default value of "Hello, and welcome" will be injected into the selfServiceWelcome field. @ConfigProperty is defined as a CDI Qualifier, as shown here.

```
1 @Qualifier
2 @Retention(RUNTIME)
3 @Target({METHOD, FIELD, PARAMETER, TYPE})
4 public @interface ConfigProperty {
5     String UNCONFIGURED_VALUE="org.eclipse.microprofile.config.configproperty.unconfigureddvalue";
6
7     @Nonbinding
8     String name() default "";
9
10    @Nonbinding
11    String defaultValue() default UNCONFIGURED_VALUE;
12 }
13
```

Line 1 declares the annotation ConfigProperty as a qualifier. Lines 8 and 10 both declare the two parameters of the annotation—name and defaultValue. As you can see, the @ConfigProperty annotation is a plain CDI qualifier that the MicroProfile Config API leverages to help externalize application configuration.

The use of @ConfigProperty is static in the sense that the values do not change even when the values change in the source of the configuration. So in this example, even if the value of the self-service config property entry changes, the injected field might not necessarily change. To truly get dynamic config values, you can use another CDI construct with the Config API, as shown next.

```
1    @Inject
2    @ConfigProperty(name = "dynamic-value")
3    private Provider<String> myDynamicValue;
```

Lines 1 and 2 use @Inject and @ConfigProperties on the myDynamicValue field. The type of myDyanmicValue, however, is a Provider from the CDI API, defined as shown next.

```
1 public interface Provider<T> {
2     T get();
3 }
```

Provider is a parameterized interface from the CDI API that has one method, get(). It returns the parameterized type. As used in the earlier code, setting the type of myDynamicValue to Provider means any time you call the get() method on it, a new instance of type String is returned with a possibly updated value from the config source. The following code snippet shows the get() method invocation on myDynamicValue to be logged.

```
1     @PostConstruct
2     private void init() {
3         Logger.getAnonymousLogger().log(Level.INFO, myDynamicValue.get());
4     }
5
```

The entire MicroProfile project is built on the Jakarta EE platform and as such, it leverages the power of the platform to help you craft cloud-native enterprise Java applications.

Apache Delta Spike

Delta Spike is an Apache top-level project that has modules in the form of CDI extensions that provide additional functionality for your Jakarta EE application. Some of the modules include the JSF, Scheduler, Security, and Data. This section examines the Data module.

The Data module provides capabilities for implementing repository patterns and thereby simplifying the repository layer. Repository patterns are ideal for simple queries that require boilerplate code, enabling centralization of query logic and consequently reducing code duplication and improving testability.[3]

For the restaurant application, you can convert the `ApplicationUser` bean to a JPA entity, as shown here.

```
1 @Entity
2 public class ApplicationUser {
3
4     @Id
5     @GeneratedValue(strategy = GenerationType.AUTO)
6     private Long id;
7
8     private String userName;
9     private String email;
10    private String address;
11    private String mobileNumber;
12    private String hashedPassword;
13
14 }
15
```

The `ApplicationUser` entity has a number of fields that, in a typical database-driven application, you would want to query on. For instance, you might want to find a user by `userName`, run another query to search by

---

[3]https://deltaspike.apache.org/documentation/data.html

email, and so on. The Delta Spike module helps you reduce such tedious boilerplate code by using CDI-based repositories. You can declare an ApplicationUserRepo that will handle the basic CRUD on the fields of the entity class for you.

```
1 @Repository
2 public interface ApplicationUserRepo
3    extends EntityRepository<ApplicationUser, Long> {
4 }
```

Line 1 declares the @Repository annotation from the Delta Spike data module on the ApplicationUserRepo interface, which extends the parameterized EntityRepository, which is also from the same Delta Spike data module. The EntityRepository interface is defined as follows:

```
 1 public interface EntityRepository<E, PK extends Serializable>
 2 {
 3
 4     E save(E entity);
 5
 6     void remove(E entity);
 7
 8     void refresh(E entity);
 9
10     void flush();
11
12     E findBy(PK primaryKey);
13
14     List<E> findAll();
15
16     List<E> findBy(E example, SingularAttribute<E, ?>... attributes);
17
18     List<E> findByLike(E example, SingularAttribute<E, ?>... attributes);
19
20     Long count();
21
22     Long count(E example, SingularAttribute<E, ?>... attributes);
23
24     Long countLike(E example, SingularAttribute<E, ?>... attributes);
25
26 }
```

This interface has some basic CRUD-based methods that almost every database application implements. For instance, Line 12 declares a findBy() method that takes the primary key of an entity and queries the database for it. All of these methods are implemented by the data module CDI extension. Next, you'll declare some methods in the interface for CRUD purposes.

```
1 @Repository
2 public interface ApplicationUserRepo
3   extends EntityRepository<ApplicationUser, Long> {
4
5     ApplicationUser findByEmail(String email);
6
7     ApplicationUser findByUserName(String userName);
8
9     Optional<ApplicationUser> findOptionalByHashedPassword(String hashedPassword);
10
11    Collection<ApplicationUser> findByUserNameLike(String userName);
12 }
```

Line 5 declares a findByEmail method. This method will search for a user by their email. Lines 7, 9, and 11 declare the findByUserName, findOptionalByHashedPassword, and findByUserNameLike methods, respectively. To use the repository, you just inject it into your QuerySerivce class, as shown here.

```
1 @CDIService
2 public class QueryService {
3
4       @Inject
5       private ApplicationUserRepo repo;
6 }
```

Line 5 declares a CDI-injected field of type ApplicationUserRepo into the QueryService class. With this, you can implement most of the tedious CRUD boilerplate code without having to write a fraction of it, as shown next.

```
 1 @CDIService
 2 public class QueryService {
 3
 4     @Inject
 5     private ApplicationUserRepo repo;
 6
 7     public ApplicationUser find(Long id) {
 8         return repo.findBy(id);
 9     }
10
11     public Optional<ApplicationUser> findOptional(Long id) {
12         return repo.findOptionalBy(id);
13     }
14
15     public ApplicationUser findByEmail(@Email String email) {
16         return repo.findByEmail(email);
17     }
18
19     public ApplicationUser findByUserName(String userName) {
20         return repo.findByUserName(userName);
21     }
22
23     public Optional<ApplicationUser> findOptionalByPassword(String hashedPassword) {
24         return repo.findOptionalByHashedPassword(hashedPassword);
25     }
26
27     public Collection<ApplicationUser> findAllByUserName(String userNamePattern) {
28         return repo.findByUserNameLike(userNamePattern);
29     }
30
31     List<ApplicationUser> findAll() {
32         return repo.findAll();
33     }
34
35
36 }
```

QueryService has a number of method declarations that use the
ApplicationUserRepo injected on Line 5. As you can see, some of the
methods are being used directly from the EntityRepository, such as the
findOptionalBy() method, which takes the ID of an entity and returns
an Optional object typed to the entity. The findAll method also invokes
the findAll method, which is found directly on the EntityRepository
interface.

All of these methods are implemented on your behalf using a
combination of CDI API constructs. For instance, the Delta Spike module
requires a producer field of type EntityManager in order to be able

to intercept and implement repository methods. The EntityManager producer method suffices for the requirement.

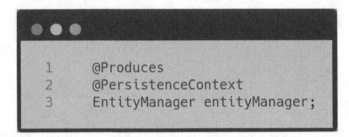

```
1       @Produces
2       @PersistenceContext
3       EntityManager entityManager;
```

The repository can also be used for persisting into the database. Remember it comes with a save() method that takes an entity and persists or merges it into the persistent context, depending on the state of the entity. You can use ApplicationUserRepo in your persistence service to persist ApplicationUser entities.

```
1 @Stateless
2 public class PersistenceService {
3
4     @Inject
5     @CreateUserQualifier
6     Event<ApplicationUser> emailEvent;
7
8     @Inject
9     private ApplicationUserRepo repo;
10
11     public ApplicationUser persistUser(ApplicationUser applicationUser) {
12         //Persist new user into datastore, returning the persisted user.
13
14         ApplicationUser savedUser = repo.save(applicationUser);
15         emailEvent.fire(savedUser);
16
17
18         return savedUser;
19
20     }
21 }
```

PersistenceService is a stateless EJB that declares a dependency on ApplicationUserRepo on Line 9. Then in the persistUser method, on Line 14, the injected repository is used to persist an ApplicationUser entity. The save() method on the repository is also automatically intercepted and implemented by the Delta Spike module on your behalf.

Afterword

As you have seen, the Contexts and Dependency Injection API is a deceptively simple yet powerful toolkit that helps you craft maintainable code and large applications. You can also count on the CDI ecosystem for helpful extensions that make your life as a Jakarta EE developer very convenient and productive. You have seen two such extensions—the Eclipse MicroProfile Config API and Apache Delta Spike—that you can immediately start using in your projects.

Whew! What a ride. This book covered all that you need to know to use the CDI API in your own code. It is impossible to cover everything about any given library in a book. However, with what you have learned up to this point, you should have a solid foundation on which you can explore the CDI spec[1] on your own.

If you need further help with any of the topics covered in this book, or you would like me to help you out with a project, or simply hangout for coffee, please do not hesitate to reach out to me at hello@pedanticacademy.com. I would love to hear from you and will respond to all your mails.

Thank you for reading this book. I appreciate your interest.

---

[1] http://docs.jboss.org/cdi/spec/2.0/cdi-spec.pdf

© Luqman Saeed 2020
L. Saeed, *Introducing Jakarta EE CDI*, https://doi.org/10.1007/978-1-4842-5642-8

Index

A, B

Apache Delta Spike
  ApplicationUser bean, 80
  defined, 80
  EntityManager, 83, 84
  EntityRepository interface, 81
  QueryService class, 82, 83
  save() method, 85
Application server, 2, 7, 8

C

CDI bean lifecycle callbacks
  interceptors, 55–59
  @PostConstruct, 53, 54
  @PreDestroy, 55
CDI beans *vs.* contextual
  instances, 23
CDI stereotypes, 71–73
Constructor injection, 34–36
Contexts and Dependency
  Injection (CDI), 75
  activation, 20–22
  annotation, 21
  @ApplicationScoped, 25, 26
  async events, 63–65
  bean creation, 24

bean lifecycle callbacks (*see* CDI
  bean lifecycle callbacks)
beans *vs.* contextual
  instances, 23
container, 22
@ConversationScoped, 29–31
default activation scope, 20
dependent pseudo-scope,
  31, 32
injection point
  constructor, 34–35
  field, 32–33
  method, 34
managed beans, 35, 36
method producers, 48–51
producer fields, 52, 53
qualifying events, 65–68
@RequestScoped, 26, 27
session beans, 36, 37
@SessionScoped, 28
synchronous events, 59–63
transactional event
  observers, 68–70

D

Dependency injection (DI), 19
Devoxx, 16

Printed in the United States
By Bookmasters